My Body

My Brain

Sally Hewitt

QED Publishing

Copyright © QED Publishing 2008
First published in the UK in 2008 by
QED Publishing
A Quarto Group company
226 City Road
London ECIV 2TT

www.qed-publishing.co.uk

A catalogue record for this book is
available from the British Library.

ISBN 978 1 84538 936 9

Printed and bound in

Author Sally Hewitt
Consultant Terry Jennings
Project Editor Judith Millidge
Designer Kim Hall
Picture Researcher Claudia Tate
Illustrator Chris Davidson

Publisher Steve Evans
Creative Director Zeta Davies

Picture credits
Key: t = top, m = middle, b = bottom,
l = left, r = right

Alamy Jason Smalley-Wildscape 9t
Corbis LWA-Dann Tardif 2lb, Norbert Schaefer 16
Shutterstock Gualberto Becerra 4l, kameel4u 4r,
Gelpi 5, 7b, Olga Shelego 6, Andresr 7t, Elena Elisseeva
7m, Jozsef Szasz-Fabian 9b, Ostanina Vadimovna 10,
Claudio Baldini 11mr, Cloki 11br, Cre8tive Images 11ml,
Ilya Gridnev 11t, MaxFX 11bl, Merrill Dyck 12, Aurelio 13t,
Alexander Shalamov 13b, Doug Schneider 14, Losevsky
Pavel 15b, 15t, 20b, Kisalev/Jaime Duplass 17, Maria
Wariatka 18, Thomas M Perkins 19t, Jiri Vaclavek 19b,
Kisalev Valerevich 20t, Marcel Mooij 2lt

Words in **bold** are
explained in the glossary
on page 22.

Contents

What is your brain?

Your **brain** is inside your head.
You think with this part of your body.
Your brain controls everything you do.
While you are asleep, your brain
keeps on working.

Your dreams are what you are
thinking about in your sleep.

4

Your brain tells your body to move. It tells you what you see, smell, hear, taste and touch. It even tells you if you are happy or sad.

You learn new things and remember them using your brain.

Your brain

Your brain is kept safe inside a strong box of bone in your head called your **skull**. Your brain needs to be protected because it is soft.

Your skull is just the right size and shape for your brain to sit inside. Your skull is made up of two sets of bones. The bones of your face are in one set and the other set protects your brain.

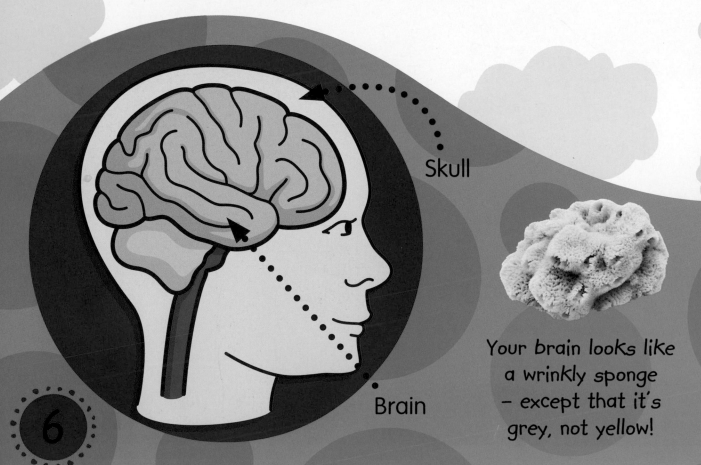

Skull

Brain

Your brain looks like a wrinkly sponge – except that it's grey, not yellow!

6

Every part of your brain has a job to do.

You think with the biggest part of your brain.

The brain stem controls digestion and makes sure your heart and breathing never stop, even when you are asleep.

The back of your brain controls how you move.

Nerves

Nerves carry **messages** from your brain to every part of your body and back again. Your nerves are like pathways. Messages run up and down them all the time.

Your spinal cord is a long tube of nerves down the middle of your back. The nerves in your spinal cord link your brain to every part of your body.

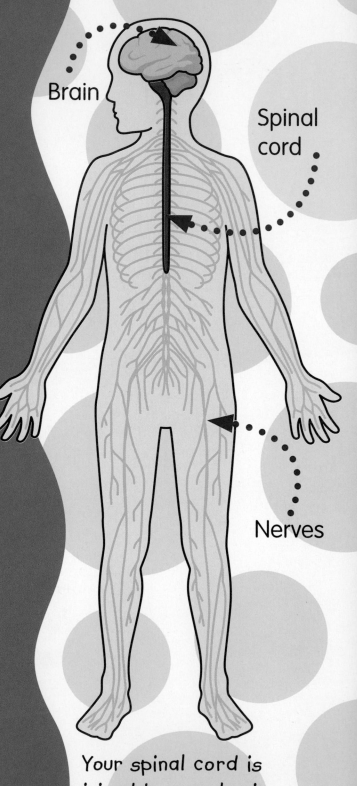

Brain

Spinal cord

Nerves

Your spinal cord is joined to your brain.

Two kinds of messages are sent along your nerves. One goes to your brain to tell it what is happening. The brain sends a reply to tell your body how to react.

This feels wet...

Pull hand out of water to get dry.

Activity

Feel something soft, such as the fur of a cat. One message tells your brain, "This feels soft!" The message that comes back tells your arm to move and your hand to stroke the cat gently.

9

Senses

Your **senses** tell you what is going on around you. You have five senses.

You *see* with your eyes.
Your *hear* with your ears.
You *smell* with your nose.
Your *taste* with your tongue.
You *feel* with your skin.

apple!

When you see something, a message is sent along your nerves from your eyes to your brain.

Your brain tells you what you are seeing.

Your senses work together to tell you things.

Your eyes see flames, your nose smells smoke, your ears hear crackling and your brain tells you "Fire!".

Your skin feels hot and warns you, "Don't touch!".

Activity

Can you tell what something is by only using one sense?

Smell an orange, soap, chocolate and a flower. Now feel them as well.

Does that help?

11

Quick as a flash!

You do some things, as quick as a flash, without thinking about them! If your finger touches a hot mug, you get the message 'hot' and quickly pull your finger away.

Are you good at hitting a ball? Your brain tells you instantly where the ball is going so you can hit it.

Activity

With a friend, drop a pencil between each other's hands. Can you catch it? Whose brain sends messages the fastest?

Memory

Your brain **remembers** things. When you taste new food for the first time, your brain remembers what it looks like, how it tastes and smells, and if you like it.

When you are given the food again, your brain remembers whether you liked it or not.

You can't remember everything, so your brain works out what is important and what is not so important.

What happened yesterday? Can you remember everything or just some important things?

Activity

It's important to remember faces. Your brain is very good at it! Find pictures of ten faces. Show five of the faces quickly to a friend. Shuffle all ten faces together. Now spread them out. Can your friend remember which of the faces he or she has already seen?

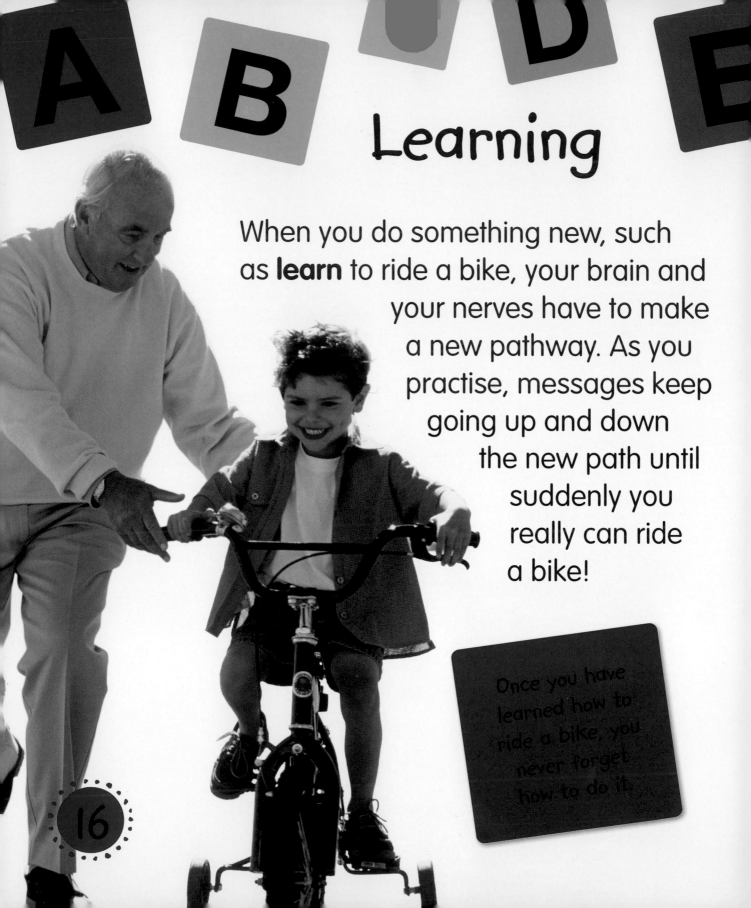

Learning

When you do something new, such as **learn** to ride a bike, your brain and your nerves have to make a new pathway. As you practise, messages keep going up and down the new path until suddenly you really can ride a bike!

Once you have learned how to ride a bike, you never forget how to do it.

16

Hard work and practice help you to learn new things, remember how to do them, and get better at doing them.

Activity

Write your name with the hand you don't usually use. Practise over and over again. Do you get better at writing with the 'wrong' hand?

17

Feelings

How do you feel when you have been invited to a sleepover with your friends? How do you feel if someone borrows your favourite pen – then loses it? Do you feel excited, angry, sad, happy?

You can usually tell how someone is feeling by the look on their face.

Your feelings come from your brain.

Activity

With your friend, think of a feeling, then pull a face and make your body show that feeling. Can your friend guess what the feeling is just by looking at you?

Feelings can help you to do the right thing at the right time.

If you feel afraid of a fierce animal, you keep away from it.

BEWARE OF THE DOG

If you feel happy to see your friend, you smile and your friend smiles back. You both feel happy and have a good time.

Healthy brain

Your brain is part of your body. There are lots of things you can do to keep it healthy.

Eat healthy food. Fruit, fish, vegetables and milk are all good for your brain, and for the rest of your body.

Having fun and chatting with friends is good for your brain.

Sport and exercise are good for your whole body, including your brain.

Your brain does not need to work as hard when you are asleep, so get plenty of sleep and let it rest.

Glossary

Brain
Your brain is inside your head. It is soft, grey and wrinkly, and it is the part of your body that controls everything you do.

Learn
You learn when you discover something new and remember it. For example, you learn to read, or to ride a bike. And you learn new facts every day.

Messages
Messages are facts and information sent from one place to another. Messages are sent along your nerves to your brain. If you see a bird, a message goes from your eyes to your brain. Your brain tells you "bird!".

Nerves
Your nerves are like pathways running from your brain to every part of your body. Messages are sent to and fro along your nerves.

Remember
When you learn a new skill, you remember it. You don't forget it and you don't have to learn it again.

Senses
You have five senses – sight, touch, taste, smell and hearing. They give you information about what is going on around you.

Skull
Your skull is the framework of bones in your head that protects your brain. It is sometimes called your brain box.

Notes for parents and teachers

1. Point out that people are animals called humans and that all animals have brains. Try to think of another animal that can talk. You could discuss the difference between a parrot talking and a human talking. Are there any other animals that can read and write?

2. Identify where your brain is. Talk about your skull, how it is hard and strong and the best shape to protect your brain. Look at the picture of the nervous system on page 8. Feel each other's spine and talk about how it is like a tube with the spinal cord running through the middle of it.

3. Talk about how the brain lets us sense the world around us. You can point to the parts of the body you use to see, hear, taste, smell and touch. Think of one thing you learn to do using each of your senses.

4. Play memory games together and exercise your brains. For example, say, "I went shopping and I bought some bread." The child repeats the item and adds a new one. "I went shopping and I bought some bread and some honey". Keep going and see how long your list can grow. The game stops when one of you forgets an item.

5. Learn something new together, maybe a poem or a new activity such as juggling or a tune on the recorder. Talk about what you find hard and what you find easy when learning something new.

Index